DENY HOLY
COMMUNION?

DENY HOLY COMMUNION?

Raymond Leo Cardinal Burke

CATHOLIC ACTION
FOR FAITH AND FAMILY

SAN DIEGO

Originally published under the title, "The Discipline Regarding the Denial of Holy Communion to Those Obstinately Persevering in Manifest Grave Sin" in the journal *Periodica de Re Canonica* Roma: Pontificia Università Gregoriana, vol. 96 (2007), 3-58.

Published by Catholic Action for Faith and Family
P. O. Box 910308, San Diego, CA 92191
CatholicAction.org

Catholic Action for Faith and Family is a lay organization inspired by the teachings of the Roman Catholic Church and dedicated to upholding and promoting the ideals of Christian Civilization.

Book Cover Design by ebooklaunch.com
Interior design: Monika Stout, Midnight Book Factory

Printed in the United States of America
ISBN 978-0-9816314-6-2

Table of Contents

Introduction

"The discipline [regarding the reception of Holy Communion] has never been easy to apply. But what is at stake for the Church demands the wisdom and courage of shepherds who will apply it."

During the 2004 United States presidential election campaign, some Bishops found themselves under question by other Bishops regarding the application of can. 915 of the *Code of Canon Law* in the case of Catholic politicians who publicly, after admonition, continue to support legislation favoring procured abortion and other legislation contrary to the natural moral law, for example, legislation permitting the cloning of human life for the purpose of harvesting stem cells through the destruction of artificially generated human embryos, and legislation redefining marriage to include a relationship between persons of the same sex. The gravity of the sin of procured abortion and of the sins involved in the commission of other intrinsically evil acts seemed to place the Catholic politicians among those who obstinately persevere in manifest grave sin, about whom can. 915 treats.

The discussion among the Bishops uncovered a fair amount of serious confusion regarding the discipline of can. 915. First of all, the denial of Holy Communion was repeatedly characterized as the imposition of a canonical penalty, when, in reality, it plainly articulates the responsibility of the minister of Holy Communion, ordinary or extraordinary, to deny Holy Communion to those who obstinately persevere in manifest grave sin.[1] The denial of Holy Communion can be the effect of the imposition or declaration of the canonical penalties of Excommunication and Interdict (cf. cc. 1331 §1, 2º; and 1332), but there are other cases in which Holy Communion must be denied, apart from any imposition or declaration of a canonical penalty, in order to respect the holiness of the Sacrament, to safeguard the salvation of the soul of the party presenting himself to receive Holy Communion, and to avoid scandal.

The matter in question was extensively discussed by the Bishops of the United States during their meeting in June of 2004. The statement of the United States Bishops, "Catholics in Political Life," adopted on June 18, 2004, which was the fruit of the discussion, failed to consider the clear requirement to exclude from Holy Communion those who, after appropriate admonition, obstinately persist in publicly sup-

---

[1] Card. W.H. Keeler, "Interim Reflections of the Task Force on Catholic Bishops and Catholic Politicians: Summary of Consultations," *Origins* 34 (2004), 106

porting legislation, which is contrary to the natural moral law. The statement reads:

The question has been raised as to whether the denial of Holy Communion to some Catholics in political life is necessary because of their public support for abortion on demand. Given the wide range of circumstances involved in arriving at a prudential judgment on a matter of this seriousness, we recognize that such decisions rest with the individual bishop in accord with the established canonical and pastoral principles. Bishops can legitimately make different judgments on the most prudent course of pastoral action.[2]

While the judgment regarding the disposition of the individual who presents himself to receive Holy Communion belongs to the minister of the Sacrament, the question regarding the objective state of Catholic politicians who knowingly and willingly hold opinions contrary to the natural moral law would hardly seem to change from place to place.

The question of the scandal involved does not seem to be addressed by the Statement. While concern was expressed about "circumstances in which Catholic teaching and sacramental practice can be misused for political ends," there is no mention of the gravely wrong conclusion that is *per se* drawn from the Church's admission of politicians, who are persistent in supporting positions and legislation which gravely violate the natural moral law, to receive Holy Communion.[3]

The Statement also seems to take away the serious responsibility of the minister of Holy Communion, resting

---

[2] US Conference of Catholic Bishops, "Catholics in Political Life," *Origins* 34 (2004), 99

[3] US Conference of Catholic Bishops, "Catholics in Political Life" (cf. nt. 2), 99

the matter entirely with the Bishop. One bishop issued a statement on the same day as the statement of the body of Bishops, which intimated that can. 915 is not to be applied in his diocese. He stated:

The archdiocese will continue to follow church teaching, which places the duty of each Catholic to examine their consciences as to their worthiness to receive Holy Communion. That is not the role of the person distributing the body and blood of Christ.[4]

The statement of the bishop in question confuses the norm of can. 916, which applies to the self-examination of the individual communicant, with the norm of can. 915, which obliges the minister of Holy Communion to refuse the Sacrament in the cases indicated.

Other bishops issued statements questioning the denial of the Holy Eucharist on the grounds that it somehow contradicts the whole nature of the Eucharist itself, asserting that the practice transforms the celebration of the Sacrament of unity into a theater of conflict.[5]

In the midst of what must objectively be called confusion, it seems best to study the history of the legislation articulated in can. 915 in order to understand the Church's constant practice and the mind of Pope John Paul II, the legislator of the 1983 *Code of Canon Law.*

---

[4] Card. R. Mahony, "Catholic Politicians and Holy Communion," *Origins* 34 (2004), 110

[5] Card. T. McCarrick, "Interim Reflections of the Task Force on Catholic Bishops and Catholic Politicians," *Origins* 34 (2004), 108; Bishop F.J. Gossman, "The State of the Soul of Those Presenting Themselves for Communion," *Origins* 34 (2004), 190

1 Corinthians 11:27-29
and *Ecclesia de Eucharistia*

The canonical discipline in question has its source in the Word of God. In the *First Letter to the Corinthians,* Saint Paul addressed the question of unworthiness to receive the Body and Blood of Christ. First, he gives an account of the institution of the Holy Eucharist, in which the teaching on the Eucharist as Sacrifice and Real Presence is clear (1 Cor 11:23-26). He then admonishes the disciples to examine their consciences before approaching to receive Holy Communion. He states:

> Whoever, therefore, eats the bread or drinks the cup of the Lord in an unworthy manner will be guilty of profaning the body and blood of the

Lord. Let a man examine himself, and so eat of the bread and drink of the cup. For anyone who eats and drinks without discerning the body eats and drinks judgment upon himself (1 Cor 11:27-29).[6]

The relationship between the teaching on the Holy Eucharist as Sacrifice and Real Presence, and the admonition regarding the correct disposition for reception of the Holy Eucharist is clear in the text.

To receive Holy Communion unworthily is to sin against Christ Himself. One commentator observed:

> The focus remains on *Christ, and Christ crucified,* as proclaimed through a self-involving sharing in the bread and wine. If stance and lifestyle make this empty of content and seriousness, participants will be *held accountable for so treating the body and blood of the Lord.*[7]

In approaching to receive the Sacrament of the Body and Blood of Christ, the faithful must both respect the holiness of the Sacrament, the Real Presence of Christ, and examine their own worthiness, lest they condemn themselves by receiving the Lord unworthily.

The emphasis is on self-examination to discover preparedness to receive the Sacrament or not. If one is not prepared, for example, because of serious sin which is unremitted, then he simply is not to approach to receive Holy Communion.

---

[6] The translation is from the *Revised Standard Version, Second Catholic Edition*

[7] A.C. Thiselton, *The First Epistle to the Corinthians: A Commentary on the Greek Text*, Grand Rapids (Michigan) 2000, 890. Cf. G.J. Lockwood, *1 Corinthians*, Saint Louis 2000, 406; and A *Catholic Commentary on Holy Scripture*, New York 1953, 1093-1094

Here, one is dealing with what may be simply called a "reality check." Does the actual state of my soul dispose me to receive the true Body and Blood of Christ?

The self-examination necessarily has reference to one's relationship both with God and with others. Communion with Christ in His Body and Blood means putting into practice what He has taught us, namely love of God and of neighbor. Serious sin against God or against neighbor makes one unworthy to receive Holy Communion until the sin has been confessed and forgiveness received through the Sacrament of Penance.

If the lack of right disposition is serious and public, and the person, nevertheless, approaches to receive the Sacrament, then he is to be admonished and denied Holy Communion. In other words, the Church cannot remain silent and indifferent to a public offense against the Body and Blood of Christ.

Perhaps the most recent authoritative commentary on Saint Paul's teaching regarding unworthiness to receive Holy Communion is found in Pope John Paul II's Encyclical Letter *Ecclesia de Eucharistia*, "On the Eucharist in Its Relationship to the Church," issued on Holy Thursday, April 17, 2003. In Chapter Four of the Encyclical Letter, "The Eucharist and Ecclesial Communion," Pope John Paul declared:

> The celebration of the Eucharist, however, cannot be the starting point for communion; it presupposes that communion already exists, a communion which it seeks to consolidate and bring to perfection. The sacrament is an expression of this bond of communion both in its *invisible* dimension, which, in Christ and through the working of the Holy Spirit, unites us

to the Father and among ourselves, and in its *visible* dimension, which entails communion in the teaching of the apostles, in the sacraments and in the Church's hierarchical order.[8]

It is especially the invisible dimension which the discipline of can. 915 safeguards.

Regarding the invisible dimension of Communion, the Holy Father reminded us of the requirement that we be in the state of grace in order to receive Holy Communion. Making reference to 1 Cor 11:28, Pope John Paul II declared that he who desires to participate in Holy Communion must be about the daily work of growing in holiness of life, that is, in the practice of the virtues of faith, hope, and love.[9] He quoted from a homily on the *Book of the Prophet Isaiah* by Saint John Chrysostom:

> I too raise my voice, I beseech, beg and implore that no one draw near to this sacred table with a sullied and corrupt conscience. Such an act, in fact, can never be called "communion," not even were we to touch the Lord's body a thousand times over, but "condemnation," "torment" and "increase of punishment."[10]

Noting the teaching in the *Catechism of the Catholic Church* (n. 1385) and following the rule of the Council of Trent, Pope John Paul II reaffirmed that, in order to receive Holy Communion worthily, one must have confessed and been absolved of any mortal sin of which he is guilty.

---

[8] Ioannes Paulus II, Litterae Encyclicae *Ecclesia de Eucharistia* [EdeE], *AAS 95* (2003) 457, n. 35a. English translation from: Libreria Editrice Vaticana, Vatican City State

[9] EdeE, 36a

[10] EdeE, 36b

Pope John Paul II then proceeded to discuss the case of grave public sin, relating the self-judgment of unworthiness to receive to the refusal of Holy Communion to the person remaining in manifest grievous sin. He declared:

> The judgment of one's state of grace obviously belongs only to the person involved, since it is a question of examining one's conscience. However, in cases of outward conduct which is seriously, clearly, and steadfastly contrary to the moral norm, the Church, in her pastoral concern for the good order of the community and out of respect for the sacrament, cannot fail to feel directly involved. The *Code of Canon Law* refers to the situation of a manifest lack of proper moral disposition when it states that those who "obstinately persist in manifest grave sin are not to be admitted to Eucharistic communion."[11]

Pope John Paul II made it clear that the norm of can. 915 is required by the Church's teaching on the respect due to the Most Blessed Sacrament and her concern to avoid scandal in the community.

With the words, "cannot fail to feel directly involved," the Roman Pontiff clarified the obligation, on the part of the Church, to take action, when a person who remains in grievous and public sin approaches to receive Holy Communion. The obligation in question is distinct from the obligation of the person to examine his conscience regarding grave sin before approaching, which is treated in can. 916.

---

[11] EdeE, 37b

CHAPTER 2

Fathers of the
Church and Theologians

The Fathers of the Church and approved theologians have addressed the Church's serious concern that due respect be paid to the Most Blessed Sacrament, that souls not fall into the sin of sacrilege by receiving the Body and Blood of Christ unworthily, and that scandal not be given to the faithful by a careless administration of the Holy Eucharist to individuals who clearly are not rightly disposed, that is, who obstinately persevere in manifest serious sin. The just-cited text from Saint John Chrysostom, found in *Ecclesia de Eucharistia,* is an excellent example.

Saint Basil the Great, in his *First Letter on the Canons,* indicates that the man who marries his brother's wife is not to be permitted to receive Holy Communion until he separates from her.[12] He, likewise, declares that the widow who takes a husband after her sixtieth year is not to be admitted to Holy Communion, until "she will have renounced her impure passion."[13] Although little commentary is offered regarding the reason for the discipline, it seems clear that, in both cases, the reason for the prohibition is a public violation of the Church's discipline regarding marriage and the resulting scandal in the community. The aforementioned canons of Saint Basil the Great are among the fonts of can. 712 of the *Code of Canons of the Eastern Churches,* which corresponds to the discipline articulated in can. 915 of the *Code of Canon Law.*[14]

The fonts of can. 712 of the *Code of Canons of the Eastern Churches* also include a text of Saint Timothy of Alexandria, which underlines the responsibility of the minister of Holy Communion to refuse the Blessed Sacrament to a public sinner. The question is posed: Is it permitted to give Holy Communion to a heretic who presents himself to receive amidst a large crowd? Saint Timothy of Alexandria responds that it is not permitted to give Holy Communion to the heretic, even if he is not recognized in the huge crowd. He comments that the one who gives Holy Communion to the

---

[12] Basile De Cesaree, "Première Lettre sur Les Canons addressée a Amphiloque, Évêque d'Iconium," in Pontificia Commissione Per La Redazione Del Codice Di Diritto Canonico Orientale, *Fonti*, fascicolo IX, t. 2 (Les canons des Pères Grecs), Grottaferrata 1963, 125, can. 23

[13] Basile De Cesaree, "Première Lettre sur Les Canons" (cf. nt. 12), 126, can. 24. Hereafter, unless otherwise indicated, all English translations are the author's

[14] Pontificium Consilium De Legum Textibus Interpretandis, *Codex Canonum Ecclesiarum Orientalium auctoritate Ioannis Pauli Pp. II promulgatus, Fontium annotatione auctus,* Vatican City State, 1995, 259, can. 712

heretic in such a situation, that is, not recognizing the heretic in the crowd, "is not responsible because of the crowd and of his ignorance of the fact."[15] The discipline is clear. Holy Communion is to be denied to the public sinner, whether the congregation is large or small. The minister, however, is not responsible for giving the Sacrament to the known heretic whom he fails to recognize because of the size of the crowd.

Saint Augustine, in Sermon 227, preaching to the newly baptized on Easter Sunday, comments on the text of Saint Paul regarding worthy reception of Holy Communion. Giving the newly baptized a fuller catechesis on the Holy Eucharist, he instructs them:

> What is receiving unworthily? Receiving with contempt, receiving with derision. Don't let yourselves think that what you can see is of no account. What you can see passes away, but the invisible reality signified does not pass away, but remains. Look, it's received, it's eaten, it's consumed. Is the body of Christ consumed, is the Church of Christ consumed, are the members of Christ consumed? Perish the thought! Here they are being purified, there they will be crowned with the victor's laurels. So what is signified will remain eternally, although the thing that signifies it seems to pass away. So receive the sacrament in such a way that you think about yourselves, that you retain unity in your hearts, that you always fix your hearts up above. Don't

---

[15] Timothee D'Alexandrei, "Réponses canoniques aux questions qui lui furent posées par des évêques et des clercs," in Pontificia Commissione Per La Redazione Del Codice Di Diritto Canonico Orientale, *Fonti*, fascicolo IX, t. 2 (Les canons des Pères Grecs), Grottaferrata 1963, 256, can. 25

let your hope be placed on earth, but in heaven. Let your faith be firm in God, let it be acceptable to God. Because what you don't see now, but believe, you are going to see there, where you will have joy without end.[16]

Saint Augustine draws the attention of the newly baptized to the reality of the Eucharistic species, the glorious Body, Blood, Soul, and Divinity of Christ, cautioning them, lest in looking upon the species, which passes away, they fail or forget to recognize that the reality, the substance, is eternal, that is, never passes away. Saint Augustine's text recalls to mind the words of Pope John Paul II about the invisible dimension of Holy Communion, which demands that those who stubbornly remain in "manifest grave sin" be denied the Sacrament.[17]

Saint Francis of Assisi addressed the question of the indiscriminate distribution of Holy Communion in his *Letter* or *Exhortation to the Clergy*. Saint Francis, first of all, lamented the lack of care for the sacred vessels and sacred linens, which hold and touch the Body and Blood of Christ, on the part of the clergy, the ministers of Holy Communion. He, then, addressed their responsibility to attend to their own worthiness and to the right disposition of those who present themselves to receive. He declared:

And besides, many clerics reserve the Blessed

---

[16] S. Augustini Episcopi, "Sermo CCXXVII (a), In die Paschae, IV, Ad Infantes, de Sacramentis," in *Opera Omnia*, ed. Monachi Ordinis Sancti Benedicti e Congregatione S. Mauri, Paris 1865, t. V, col. 1101. English translation from Augustine of Hippo, "Sermon 227: Preached on the Holy Day of Easter to the *Infantes*, on the Sacraments," in *Sermons*, vol. III/6 (184-229Z), tr. Edmund Hill, O.P., New Rochelle 1993, 255-256

[17] EdeE, 36-37

Sacrament in unsuitable places, or carry It about irreverently, or receive It unworthily, or give It to all-comers without distinction. [18]

With regard to the reception of Holy Communion, Saint Francis underlined two solemn moral obligations of the minister of Holy Communion: first, the obligation to be personally disposed to receive the Body and Blood of Christ worthily, and second, the obligation to give Holy Communion with discretion, that is, with attention to those who, in a public way, have made themselves unworthy to receive the Sacrament.

[18] Saint Francis of Assisi, "Epistola ad clericos (Recensio prior)," in *Die Opuscula des Hl. Franziskus von Assisi,* Neue textkritische Edition, ed. Kajetan Esser, O.F.M., Grottaferrata 1976, 163-164. English translation from: *The Writings of St. Francis of Assisi,* tr. Benen Fahy, O.F.M., Chicago 1964, 101

CHAPTER 3

Decretal Law

The first legislation in the matter, collected in the *Decree of Gratian,* is a letter from Pope Gregory the Great to an elderly Bishop Januarius who was reported to have gone out to take the harvest of a certain man before the celebration of the Mass and then, to have proceeded to celebrate the Mass. The letter comments: "All who hear about the fact know that a punishment ought to follow it."[19] The case is somewhat complicated. The discipline, in fact, is not imposed upon the Bishop because of his simple-mindedness and age. Pope Gregory, however, imposed two months of excommunication upon those who counseled the Bishop to act in such a way. The letter further specifies that, if they will have suffered illness within the two months, they are not to

---

[19] C. 24, D. LXXXVI

be deprived of the blessing of Viaticum. The letter concludes by reminding the Bishop that, henceforth, he has been cautioned against the counsel of such persons.[20]

Although the norm, as is proper for legislation, does not comment on the reason for the severe discipline, it is clear that the action of Bishop Januarius was in public violation of the divine precept to avoid servile labor on the Lord's Day. Clearly, the scandal caused was greater because the sin was committed by a bishop.

The *Decree of Gratian* also quotes the discipline from the Council of Carthage that an excommunicated bishop or priest who receives Holy Communion before a hearing is judged to have passed upon himself a judgment of condemnation.[21] Once again, the case of denying Holy Communion involves a public and grave sin, which until it has been addressed through an ecclesiastical hearing, demands that the bishop or priest be refused Holy Communion.

In addition, the *Decree of Gratian* quotes the discipline of the Council of Agde or Montpellier: "And we have judged that murderers and false witnesses are to be kept from ecclesiastical communion, unless their crimes will have been absolved by the satisfaction of penitence."[22] The cases that demand refusal of Holy Communion are seen to include murder and false witness, both public acts involving grave matters. Until the guilty party has been absolved of the grave sin, his reception of Holy Communion would constitute sacrilege and would give scandal to others, confusing them regarding the sacredness of the Most Blessed Sacrament.

---

[20] C. 24, D. LXXXVI
[21] C. 9, C. XI, q. 3
[22] C. 20, C. XXIV, q. 3

In the *Decree of Gratian,* we also find a quotation from a letter of Cyprian Euricacius to a confrère, in which he responds to a request for counsel regarding the question of whether a certain charlatan and sorcerer ought to be given Holy Communion. The question refers to the fact that the person in question perseveres in the shamefulness of his art, becoming a teacher and expert for children who, because of his bad example, are not educated but are led astray.[23] It further references the truth that evil taught to some also reaches others, which seems to be a clear reference to scandal. The response is: "I think that it is neither congruent with the divine majesty or evangelical discipline, in order that the modesty and honor of the Church not be sullied by such an indecent and infamous contagion."[24]

In the *Decretals of Pope Gregory IX,* we find the decree of the Third Lateran Council, which established that "manifest usurers are not to be admitted to the communion of the altar." The decree also denied ecclesiastical burial to an unrepentant usurer, mandated that their offerings were not to be accepted, and suspended from the execution of his office the cleric who would accept their offerings until, in the judgment of his Bishop, he had returned the offerings.[25]

From the Decretal Law, it is clear that Church discipline places an obligation on the minister of Holy Communion to refuse Holy Communion to persons known, by the public, to be in mortal sin. The discipline, faithful to the teaching of Saint Paul, safeguards the recognition of the most sacred nature of the Holy Eucharist, preventing public sinners from inflicting further grave damage upon their souls through the

---

[23] C. 95, D. II, *de cons*

[24] C. 95, D. II, *de cons*

[25] C. 3, X, *de usuris*, V, 19

unworthy reception of the Holy Eucharist and safeguarding the faithful from the inevitable confusion regarding the sacredness of the Sacrament, which is caused by the admission of manifest and grave sinners to the reception of Holy Communion.

CHAPTER 4

Rituale Romanum of 1614

The *Rituale Romanum* published by Pope Paul V on June 17, 1614, presents the discipline of the Church regarding the Sacraments and sacramentals, in accord with the reforms of the Council of Trent. It was published principally for the use of priests, even as the *Pontificale Romanum* and *Caeremoniale Episcoporum* were published in 1595-1596 and 1600, respectively, for the bishops. It is a universal *vademecum* for priests in what is their principal and highest activity: the celebration of the Sacraments and sacramentals.

In the section, "On the Most Holy Sacrament of the Eucharist" *(De Sanctissimo Eucharistiae Sacramento),* the priests are reminded that the Holy Eucharist contains "the principal and greatest gift of God, Christ the Lord, the very author and font of all grace and holiness."[26] They are, therefore, urged to put forth the greatest effort in the reverence before and care of the Most Blessed Sacrament, on their own part, and in the worship and holy reception of the Sacrament, on the part of the faithful in their pastoral care. The priests are reminded of the specific instructions which they should give to the faithful in preparing to receive and in receiving Holy Communion.

The discipline regarding the reservation of the Holy Eucharist in the tabernacle and the tabernacle itself is given in detail. The parish priest is reminded that he is to take care that everything ordered to the worship of the Most Blessed Sacrament be intact and clean, and be maintained so.[27] The care of the sacred linens and vessels is a very concrete expression of the integral respect owed to the Most Blessed Sacrament, as Saint Francis of Assisi had declared in his succinct admonition to the clergy regarding the care to be given to the Holy Eucharist.

Regarding the ministering of the Sacrament to the faithful, the *Rituale Romanum* established:

> All the faithful are to be admitted to Holy Communion, except those who are prohibited for a just reason. The publicly unworthy, which are the excommunicated, those under interdict, and the manifestly infamous, such as prostitutes, those cohabiting, usurers, sorcerers, fortune-tellers, blasphemers and other sinners of the public kind, are, however, to be prevented, unless their

---

[26] *Rituale Romanum*, Editio Princeps (1614), ed. Manlio Sodi, S.D.B., and Juan Javier Flores Arcas, O.S.B., Città del Vaticano, 2004, 56

[27] *Rituale Romanum* (cf. nt. 26), 56-57

penitence and amendment has been established and they will have repaired the public scandal.[28]

The discipline by which those persevering in manifest and grievous sin are kept from receiving Holy Communion is seen as integral to the worship and care of the Holy Eucharist. The responsibility of the Church in the matter clearly rests with the priest as the minister of the Sacrament, lest the greatest good of the Church be violated, the communicant commit sacrilege, and the faithful, in general, be scandalized.

The language of the discipline reflects the language of the Decretal Law. The same language will be found in the subsequent articulation of the Church's discipline.

The *Rituale Romanum* concludes the instruction to the priests by taking up three other cases of persons to whom it may be necessary to refuse Holy Communion. The first case involves occult grievous sinners who ask for Holy Communion. If they ask occultly and the priest does not recognize them as having amended their life, he is to refuse Holy Communion to them. If, however, they publicly seek the Sacrament and the priest cannot deny the Sacrament to them without causing scandal, then he is to give Holy Communion to them.

Here, it is necessary to note two meanings of the term 'scandal' in Church discipline. The first and properly theological meaning of scandal is to do or omit something which leads others into error or sin. The second meaning is to do or omit something which causes wonderment *(admiratio)* in others. Denying Holy Communion publicly to the occult sinner involves scandal in the second sense. Giving Holy Communion to the obstinately serious and public sinner involves scandal in the first sense. The second case involves persons

---

[28] Ibid., 49

suffering from mental illness. The third case involves those who, because of senility, no longer recognize the Sacrament. [29]

In the section, "On the Communion of the Sick" *(De Communione infirmorum),* priests are urged to employ the greatest effort and diligence in providing Viaticum to the sick, lest, through the pastor's lack of attention, the sick die without the Blessed Sacrament. The priests, however, are cautioned lest, to the scandal of others, they give Holy Communion to the unworthy. The following groups of people are listed as examples of the unworthy: "public usurers; the cohabiting; the notoriously criminal, namely, the excommunicated or the denounced, unless beforehand they will have purified themselves by Holy Confession, and will have repaired, as according to the law, the public offense."[30] The discipline set forth, with its particular application to the case of the sick and the dying, is the same as that articulated in the section on the Holy Eucharist.

---

[29] Ibid

[30] Ibid., 60-61

CHAPTER 5

Pope Benedict XIV

To understand the discipline of can. 915 of the *Code of Canon Law*, it is important to review, albeit briefly, the teaching of Pope Benedict XIV, the noted canonist Prospero Lambertini, in the matter. Pope Benedict XIV served as Successor of Saint Peter from August 17, 1740, until his death on May 3, 1758. The case in which his teaching is set forth concerns the followers of Pasquier Quesnel (1634-1719).

Pope Clement XI (1700-1721), through his Constitution *Unigenitus Dei Filius* of September 8, 1713, condemned certain propositions taken from the writings of Quesnel, a French Oratorian who fell into the errors of Jansenism and Gallicanism.[31] Sadly, Quesnel refused correction and became

---

[31] *DS* 2400-2502; cf. *Codicis Iuris Canonici Fontes*, vol. I, 539-542, n. 270.

obstinate in his errors. As is not uncommon in the history of the Church, he gained a following.

Pope Benedict XIV had to address the question regarding whether adherents to the errors of Quesnel might be admitted to receive Holy Communion as Viaticum.[32] In his Encyclical Letter *Ex omnibus* to the Cardinals, Archbishops, and Bishops of the Kingdom of France *("Regni Galliarum"),* dated October 16, 1756, he responded that "inasmuch as they are publicly and notoriously obstinate before the just mentioned Constitution, it is to be denied to them; assuredly from the general rule which forbids that a public and notorious sinner be admitted to participation of Eucharistic Communion, whether he publicly or privately requests it."[33]

Pope Benedict XIV goes on to provide pastoral instructions for those ministering to a person who is believed to be obstinate in holding to Quesnel's errors. He urges a personal, calm, and understanding approach to ascertain the truth regarding the individual's conscience. If the individual holds to the errors that endanger his or her eternal salvation, the Holy Father urges the minister of Holy Communion to point out that receiving the Body of Christ will not make him secure before the tribunal of Christ but rather guilty of a new and more detestable sin because he has eaten and drunk judgment on himself.[34] The allusion is clearly to Saint Paul's *First Letter to the Corinthians* (1 Cor 11:27-29).

---

[32] Benedictus XIV, Encyclical Letter *Ex omnibus,* in *Codicis Iuris Canonici Fontes,* vol. II, 536, n. 441 §3

[33] Benedictus XIV, Encylical Letter Ex omnibus (cf. nt. 32), 536

[34] *Codicis Iuris Canonici Fontes,* vol. II, 537, n. 441 §9

CHAPTER 6

Synodal Legislation
of the Eastern Churches

The discipline regarding the denial of Holy Communion to public sinners is also clearly enunciated in the synodal legislation of the Eastern Churches. For example, in the year 1599, the Malabar Church of southern India held a synod in the city of Diamper, which was convoked by the Latin Archbishop of Goa, Alexius de Menezes.[35] Decree III of the Synod of Diamper, referring to the teaching of Saint Paul in the *First Letter to the Corinthians,* declared:

> Wherefore, it is not permitted to give this Sacrament to public sinners, until they will have given up their sins, such as are public sorcerers, pros-

---

[35] C. De Clercq, *Fontes Iuridici Ecclesiarum Orientalium: Studium Historicum,* Romae 1967, 112-113

titutes, the publicly cohabiting, and those who publicly profess hatreds without reconciliation.[36]

The decree in question also gives careful instruction regarding the vigilance of the local vicars, lest they sin gravely by offering the Sacrament to public sinners.

In 1720, the Ruthenian Church held a provincial council at Zamostia in which the Apostolic Nuncio, the metropolitan archbishop, 7 bishops, 8 major superiors of religious orders, and 129 members of the secular and regular clergy participated.[37] Regarding the denial of Holy Communion, the Synod made its own the perennial discipline of the Church:

> Lest occasion be given to some scandal or loss of good name, the Holy Eucharist is not to be denied to the unworthy sinner because of some secret sin, above all, if the priest giving Communion will have received news of it from the confession of the sinner himself, seeking publicly the Eucharist. Heretics, schismatics, the excommunicated, the interdicted, public criminals, the openly infamous, as also prostitutes, the publicly cohabiting, major usurers, fortune-tellers, and other evil-doing men of the same kind, however, are not to be admitted to the reception of this Sacrament, according to the precept of Christ: "Do not give the Holy to dogs."[38]

---

[36] "Diampertina Synodus in Malabria," in J.D.Mansi (ed.), *Sacrorum Conciliorum nova et amplissima collectio,* Graz 1961, vol. 35, col. 1238

[37] C. De Clercq, *Fontes Iuridici Ecclesiarum Orientalium: Studium Historicum,* ROMAE 1967, 112-113

[38] "Synodus Provincialis Ruthenorum habita in Civitate Zamosciae," in J.D. Mansi, *Sacrorum Conciliorum nova et amplissima collectio,* Graz 1961, vol. 35, coll. 1492-1493

The legislation seeks to safeguard the good name of the sinner whose sin is not public. The term 'scandal' is used in the second sense, that is, wonderment causing the loss of good name. At the same time, the legislation requires that the public sinner be denied Holy Communion. The Scriptural quotation is from the Sermon on the Mount (Mt 7:6). The legislation, however, makes reference to the healing of the Canaanite woman, recounted in the *Gospel according to Matthew* (15:26), underlining the necessity of integrity of faith for the reception of grace. The Canaanite woman, in fact, because of her faith was the recipient of the healing grace of our Lord. The person who persists in grave and public sin lacks the integrity of faith, which is required to receive the Sacrament.

Regarding the discipline of the Eastern Churches in the matter, the legislation of the Synod of the Maronites of 1736, confirmed *"in forma specifica"* by Pope Benedict XIV on September 1, 1741, is most instructive. The legislation of the Synod of 1736 is the principal font of the canonical legislation of Catholics of the Maronite Rite and is also a font of can. 712 of the *Code of Canons of the Eastern Churches*.[39]

Regarding Holy Communion, the Synod of 1736 legislated that the "publicly unworthy" are not to be admitted to Holy Communion. The legislation gives as examples of those to be denied Holy Communion the following: "heretics, schismatics, apostates, the excommunicated, the interdicted, and the openly notorious, such as prostitutes, the cohabiting, usurers, sorcerers, fortune-tellers, blasphemers and other sinners of this public kind." The legislation gives two

---

[39] Sacra Congregazione Orientale, Codificazione Canonica Orientale, Fonti, fascicolo XII (Disciplina Antiochena: Maroniti), I (Ius Particulare Maronitarum), Vatican City State, 1933, vii

29

conditions under which they may subsequently be admitted to receive Holy Communion: 1) the establishment of their penance and change of life; and 2) the prior repair of public scandal.[40] In other words, the canonical discipline is directed both to the eternal salvation of the soul of the sinner and to the correction of the scandal given by a person who publicly violates the moral law in a grave matter and then presumes to receive Holy Communion.

---

[40] *Syn. Lib. II, XII*, 12, 245-246

CHAPTER 7

Responses of the Dicasteries of the Roman Curia

The understanding of the canonical discipline regarding the refusal of Holy Communion is also illustrated through the responses of the Dicasteries of the Roman Curia in the matter. For example, on April 29, 1784, the Sacred Congregation of the Propagation of the Faith issued an instruction to the Apostolic Vicariate of Soochow, addressing several pastoral questions of missionaries in China.

One of the questions concerned the withholding of Holy Communion from those who had confessed and repented of their sins but, in the judgment of the missionaries, were not sufficiently disposed to receive the Most Blessed Sacrament. The Instruction takes due note of the fitting preparation that is required for the reception of Holy Communion, making allusion to Saint Paul's *First Letter to the Corinthians.*

After providing direction for the missionaries, drawn especially from the teaching of the Council of Trent, the Instruction makes reference to the section of the *Roman Ritual* on the Holy Eucharist, which prohibited the giving of Holy Communion to those guilty of scandalous behavior, namely, "drunks, usurers, the impure, the sacrilegious, the disturbers of the peace, the inconstant in faith, hypocrites, those who hand over their daughters for marriage to the unbaptized, the scandalous, and others who are contaminated by the more serious shameful acts."[41] The Instruction goes on to ask the question:

> But, if pitiable and completely defiled men of this type have truly and soundly repented of their sins; if they will have carried out those remedies, given to them by confessors, for the conversion of life, the restitution of stolen goods and the repair of scandal, according to the above-given rules, and moreover will have shown the worthy fruits of penitence, by which they also hope for forgiveness from God, and nothing prohibits the request of the absolution of their crimes by the priest penitentiary, why would they not be admitted to Eucharistic Communion?[42]

To be noted here are the requirements of true conversion: restitution in the case of sins against the Seventh Commandment and the repair of scandal.

On December 10, 1860, the Sacred Apostolic Penitentiary published a number of responses to serious pastoral questions. Question n. 20 read: "Whether the Most Blessed

---

[41] *Codicis Iuris Canonici Fontes*, vol. VII, 143, n. 4598

[42] Ibid., vol. VII, 144, n. 4598

Eucharist may be given to those who are notoriously bound by censure, unless, as is fitting, they first will have been reconciled with the Church?"[43] The response is negative.

Although no explanation of the response is given, one has to suppose that three reasons underlie the response: the most sacred nature of the Sacrament of the Holy Eucharist, the serious sin committed by a public sinner who would receive Holy Communion without repenting of his sin, and the grave scandal caused by giving Holy Communion to a member of the faithful notoriously bound by censure, who has not been reconciled.

On July 27, 1892, the Sacred Congregation of the Holy Office responded to the question: "Whether it is permitted to administer the sacraments of the dying to the faithful who certainly do not adhere to the Masonic sect and are not led by its principles, but, moved by other reasons, have ordered their bodies to be cremated after death, if they refuse to retract the order?"[44] The response given was: "If, having been warned, they refuse, No. As to whether or not a warning should be given, the rules handed on by the proven authors are to be followed, taking into account, above all, the need to avoid scandal."[45]

The response centers upon the correction of a wrongly formed conscience before the denial of Holy Communion. It rightly requires that scandal be avoided.

On July 1, 1949, the Supreme Sacred Congregation of the Holy Office issued a decree in response to four questions regarding the involvement of Catholics with the Communist Party. The third question was: "Whether Christ's

---

[43] Ibid., vol. VIII, 456, n. 6426

[44] Ibid., vol. IV, 479, n. 1158

[45] Ibid

faithful, who have knowingly and freely performed the acts treated in nos. 1 and 2, may be admitted to the Sacraments."[46] The acts treated in the first two questions were: "whether it would be lawful to join the Communist Party or to offer support to it" and "whether it would be lawful to edit, distribute or read books, periodicals, journals or manuscripts, which support the teaching or action of Communists, or to write in them."[47]

The response to the third question was: "To 3. *No*, according to the ordinary principles of denying the Sacraments to those who are not disposed."[48] In the response to the first question, the reason why those who cooperate, in some formal way, with the Communist Party are not disposed to receive the Sacraments is provided. The response explains:

> For Communism is materialistic and anti-Christian; the leaders of the Communist Party, moreover, even if at times they declare that they do not oppose Religion, in truth, they show themselves, both by teaching and by action, to be inimical to God, to true Religion, and to the Church of Christ.[49]

The discipline, in particular, indicates that among the categories of persons who are to be denied Holy Communion are those who publicly espouse political doctrines that are hostile to the Faith and to the Church. In a similar way, those who publicly support political platforms or legislative agendas which are gravely contrary to the natural moral law show that

---

[46] Suprema Sacra Congregatio S. Officii, "II, Decretum 1 Iulii 1949," *AAS* 41 (1949) 334

[47] Ibid., "II, Decretum 1 Iulii 1949" (cf. nt. 46), 334

[48] Ibid

[49] Ibid

they are not rightly disposed to receive Holy Communion.

On November 26, 1983, the Congregation for the Doctrine of the Faith issued a declaration regarding Masonic associations, with the approval of Pope John Paul II who ordered its publication. The Declaration responded to the question of whether the judgment of the Church had changed regarding Masonic associations since they are not expressly mentioned in the 1983 *Code of Canon Law,* as they were in the 1917 *Code of Canon Law.* The response given in the Declaration contains four points: 1) the Church's negative judgment regarding Masonic associations remains unchanged because the principles of the associations are irreconcilable with the Church's teaching; 2) membership, therefore, in them remains forbidden; 3) members of the faithful who join Masonic associations fall into serious sin; and 4) "they may not approach for Holy Communion."[50] Referring to the Congregation's declaration of February 17, 1981, the Declaration further indicates that local ecclesiastical authorities do not enjoy the faculty "of offering a judgment regarding the nature of Masonic associations, which would involve the derogation of the above-stated judgment."[51]

Before the meeting of the United States Conference of Catholic Bishops in June of 2004, various Bishops had spoken and written about the application of can. 915 in the case of Catholic politicians who, after being duly admonished, publicly persist in supporting legislation grievously contrary to the natural moral law. A certain and, in some cases, serious diversity of judgment in the matter became evident among the Bishops. In early June, in order to assist the Bishops,

[50] Sacra Congregatio Pro Doctrina Fidei, "Declaratio de associationibus massonicis," *AAS* 76 (1984), 300

[51] Ibid. (cf. nt. 50), 300

Cardinal Joseph Ratzinger sent a memorandum, entitled "Worthiness to Receive Holy Communion," to Cardinal Theodore McCarrick who was exercising leadership in the Conference of Bishops regarding matters of domestic policy. The Memorandum sets forth six "general principles" concerning worthiness to receive Holy Communion.

The first principle reads: "Presenting oneself to receive Holy Communion should be a conscious decision, based on a reasoned judgment regarding one's worthiness to do so, according to the Church's objective criteria."[52] It further declares: "The practice of indiscriminately presenting oneself to receive Holy Communion merely as a consequence of being present at Mass is an abuse that must be corrected."[53]

The second principle quotes nos. 73 and 74 of the Encyclical Letter *Evangelium Vitae,* in which Pope John Paul II sets forth the Church's perennial moral teaching forbidding, always and everywhere, formal cooperation in intrinsically evil acts. With respect to the activity of legislatures and courts, the principle makes it clear that Catholics must oppose "judicial decisions or civil laws that authorize or promote abortion or euthanasia."[54]

The third principle underlines the diversity of moral weight between abortion and euthanasia, on the one hand, and war and the death penalty, on the other. The Memorandum declares: "There may be a legitimate diversity of opinion even among Catholics about waging war and applying the

---

[52] "Vatican, U.S. Bishops: On Catholics in Political Life," *Origins* 34 (2004), 133

[53] Ibid. (cf. nt. 52), 133

[54] Ibid

death penalty, but not however with regard to abortion and euthanasia."[55]

The fourth principle distinguishes between the judgment that the individual must make about his worthiness and the discretion which the minister of Holy Communion must employ regarding those who present themselves to receive the Sacrament. The principle calls to mind that "the minister of Holy Communion may find himself in the situation where he must refuse to distribute Holy Communion to someone, such as in cases of a declared excommunication, a declared interdict or an obstinate persistence in manifest grave sin."[56]

The fifth principle provides instruction for the pastor regarding the handling of a case of obstinate persistence in public serious sin. It refers explicitly to the case of Catholic politicians:

> Regarding the grave sin of abortion or euthanasia, when a person's formal cooperation becomes manifest (understood, in the case of a Catholic politician, as his consistently campaigning and voting for permissive abortion and euthanasia laws), his pastor should meet with him, instructing him about the Church's teaching, informing him that he is not to present himself for Holy Communion until he brings to an end the objective situation of sin and warning him that he will otherwise be denied the Eucharist.[57]

The principle makes clear the application of can. 915 to the case of a Catholic politician who persists in publicly supporting legislation in grave violation of the natural moral

---

[55] Ibid., 133-134

[56] Ibid., 134

[57] Ibid

37

law. It also provides the pastoral instruction regarding the procedure to be followed in observing the norm of the law in the matter.

The sixth principle, making reference to a declaration of the Pontifical Council for Legislative Texts of June 4, 2000, declares that, when a person who has been duly admonished persists in presenting himself for Holy Communion, the minister of Holy Communion must refuse to give the Sacrament. The principle further clarifies that the decision of the minister of Holy Communion "is not a sanction or a penalty" but rather the recognition of objective and public unworthiness to receive Holy Communion.[58]

The Memorandum has an appended note regarding the situation of the Catholic who would deliberately vote for a candidate "precisely because of the candidate's permissive stand on abortion and/or euthanasia."[59] It also states the applicable moral principles governing the action of a Catholic who "does not share a candidate's stand in favor of abortion and/or euthanasia, but votes for that candidate for other reasons."[60]

On July 9, 2004, Cardinal Joseph Ratzinger wrote a letter to Cardinal Theodore McCarrick who had forwarded to him a copy of the statement of the United States Conference of Catholic Bishops, "Catholics in Political Life," adopted on June 18, 2004. The letter declared:

> The statement is very much in harmony with the general principles "Worthiness to Receive Holy Communion," sent as a fraternal service – to

---

[58] Ibid

[59] Ibid

[60] Ibid

clarify the doctrine of the Church on this specific issue – in order to assist the American Bishops in their related discussion and determinations.[61]

The letter does not offer further comment on "Catholics in Political Life."

CHAPTER 8

The Pio-Benedictine Code of Canon Law (1917)

T he question of those to be excluded from the reception of Most Holy Communion is treated in can. 855 of the 1917 *Code of Canon Law*. The canon reads:

> Can.855 §1. The publicly unworthy, who are the excommunicated, the interdicted and the manifestly infamous, unless their penance and conversion have been established and they will have first made up for the public scandal, are to be excluded from the Eucharist.
>
> §2. The minister is also to refuse occult sinners, if they request secretly and he will not have recognized them as converted; not, however, if

they publicly request and he is not able to pass over them without scandal.[62]

Father Felice Cappello, S.J., noted commentator on the Pio-Benedictine Code, describes the principle which underlies the discipline of can. 855. He reminds us that the minister of Holy Communion is held, under pain of mortal sin, to deny the sacraments to the unworthy, that is, "to those who are indeed a capable subject of the sacrament, but are not able to receive its effect, because they are in the state of mortal sin without the will of reforming themselves."[63]

Basing himself on Saint Thomas Aquinas and Saint Alphonsus Liguori, Father Cappello goes on to explain the reason for the discipline:

> The *dignity* itself of the sacraments and the *virtue of religion* demand it, lest sacred things be exposed to profanation; the *fidelity* of the minister demands it, who is forbidden to give holy things to the dogs and to throw pearls before the swine; the *law of charity* demands it, lest the minister cooperate with those who unworthily attempt and dare to receive the sacraments, and offer scandal.[64]

Father Cappello clearly summarizes the certain elements of the canonical discipline regarding the denial of Holy Communion before the codification of 1917. The sublime reality of the Sacrament demands that it not be subjected to profanation by unworthy reception. The responsibility of

---

[62] Can. 855. Pio-Benedictine Code, 1917

[63] F.M. Cappello, *Tractatus canonico-moralis de Sacramentis,* vol. I, 7th ed., Turin 1962, 48, n. 58

[64] F.M. Cappello, *Tractatus canonico-moralis de Sacramentis* (cf. nt. 53), 48

the minister of Holy Communion demands that he not give the Sacrament indiscriminately to those who are not rightly disposed. Pastoral charity requires that Holy Communion be denied for the sake of the salvation of the person wrongly presenting himself to receive and for the sake of those who would be led astray regarding the truth of the Sacrament and the requirements for worthy reception.

CHAPTER 9

1983 Code of Canon Law

I n order to understand the mind of the Legislator of
the *Code of Canon Law* of 1983, it is necessary to review
the work of the Pontifical Commission for the Revision
of the Code of Canon Law, appointed by the Roman Pontiff
to assist him in his responsibility as legislator. Regarding the
discipline contained in can. 855 of the 1917 *Code of Canon
Law,* the first proposal for the text of the legislation read:

> They who have sinned grievously and man-
> ifestly remain in contumacy are not to be
> admitted to the celebration of the Most Holy
> Eucharist or to Communion.[65]

---

[65] Pontificia Commissio Codici Iuris Canonici Recognoscendo, *Schema
Documenti Pontificii quo Disciplina Canonica de Sacramentis Recognoscitur,*
Vatican City State, 1975, can. 75

The proposed canon was discussed by the Special Committee on the Sacraments *(Coetus specialis de Sacramentis)* at its meeting from May 29 to June 2 of 1978.[66] Cardinal Pericle Felici, President of the Commission, the then Archbishop Rosalio I. Castillo Lara, Secretary of the Commission, and Monsignor Willy Onclin, Adjunct Secretary of the Commission, were present. Father Mariano De Nicolò took the minutes of the meeting.

The first observation regarding the discipline sought to provide for the reception of Holy Communion by the divorced and remarried. All the Consultors of the Commission responded that it was not the work of the Commission to treat such matters and that it would be for the Holy See to respond to the observation.[67]

Secondly, the words referring to the celebration of the Most Holy Eucharist were removed, because the canon treats of participation in the Holy Eucharist. It was observed that exclusion from the celebration carries with it the nature of a punishment and, therefore, is treated in the penal law. The removal of the reference to the celebration was also seen to respect the title of the section, namely, "Regarding Participation in the Most Holy Eucharist."[68] Finally, the words "and publicly" were added after "grievously."[69]

The discipline in question appeared as canon 867 in the 1980 Schema of the *Code of Canon Law* and read:

> They who have grievously and publicly sinned, and manifestly remain in contumacy are not to

---

[66] Cf. Communicationes 13 (1981), 408-425

[67] Ibid., 412

[68] Ibid., 412-413

[69] Ibid., 413

be admitted to Holy Communion.[70]

The observations presented by the Fathers of the Commission and the responses from the Secretariat and Consultors of the Commission are indicated in the *Report Including the Synthesis of the Observations by the Most Eminent and Most Excellent Fathers of the Commission to the Latest Schema of the Code of Canon Law, with the Responses Given by the Secretary and by the Consultors.*[71] The section of the Observations regarding the Sanctifying Office of the Church is also found in *Communicationes* 15 (1983) 170-253; the observations regarding can. 867 are found on page 194.

Regarding can. 867, one of the Fathers, namely Cardinal Ermenegildo Florit of Florence, indicated that he found the text too generic in relation to can. 1135 of the Schema. Canon 1135, in Chapter 2, "On Those to be Granted and to Be Denied Ecclesiastical Burial," of the Second Title, "On Ecclesiastical Burial," of the 1980 Schema read:

§1. They are to be deprived of ecclesiastical burial, unless before death they will have given some signs of repentance:

1. notorious apostates, heretics and schismatics;

2. who have chosen the cremation of their body for reasons adverse to the Christian faith;

---

[70] Codex Iuris Canonici: *Schema Patribus Commissionis Reservatum*, E Civitate Vaticana 1980, can. 867

[71] Pontificia Commissio Codici Iuris Canonici Recognoscendo, *Relatio complectens synthesim animadversionum ab Em.mis atque Exc.mis Patribus Commissionis ad novissimum schema Codicis Iuris Canonici exhibitarum, cum responsionibus a Secretaria et Consultoribus datis*, E Civitate Vaticana, 1981, 214

> 3. other manifest sinners to whom eccle-
> siastical burial cannot be granted without
> the public scandal of the faithful.
>
> §2. When there is any doubt, the Ordinary of the
> place is to be consulted, whose judgment is to be
> followed.[72]

Cardinal Florit also urged that attention be given to can. 855 of the Pio-Benedictine *Code of Canon Law*.

Can. 1135 §1 of the 1980 Schema provides examples of those who are to be denied ecclesiastical burial, as can. 855 §1 of the 1917 *Code* provides examples of those who are to be denied reception of Holy Communion. Although Cardinal Florit's observation is not further elaborated, it seems that he was asking that the canon on the refusal of Holy Communion to those who persist in public and grievous sin should give examples, as can. 1135 §1 of the 1980 Schema and can. 855 §1 do.

Cardinal Pietro Palazzini observed that can. 855 of the Pio-Benedictine *Code of Canon Law* had been too tempered in the matter. He further objected that the scandal, which can. 855 §2 of the 1917 Code treats, was not considered, in any manner, by the proposed text. It should be noted that the term "scandal" in can. 855 §2 is used in the second, not properly theological, sense; that is, wonderment *(admira-tio)* causing loss of good name.

The response given to both observations was:

> The text suffices for it contains all of the
> requirements: namely, gravity of the act, the
> public nature of the act, and contumacy. Most

---

[72] Codex Iuris Canonici: Schema Patribus Commissionis Reservatum, E Civitate Vaticana: Libreria Editrice Vaticana, 1980, can. 1135

certainly the text refers also to the divorced and remarried.[73]

The response seemingly does not address, in any way, the request of a list of some of those to be denied the Sacrament. The question of scandal, in either of the senses noted above, is not addressed.

The text of the discipline in the 1982 draft of the *Code of Canon Law* appears in can. 913. The 1982 draft was prepared after consultation with the Cardinals of the Holy Roman Church, the Conferences of Bishops, the Dicasteries of the Roman Curia, the Faculties of Ecclesiastical Universities, and the Superiors of Institutes of the Consecrated Life. It had been revised at the pleasure of the Fathers of the Commission and had been presented to Pope John Paul II. Can. 913 reads:

> The excommunicated and interdicted after the imposition or declaration of the penalty and others who remain obstinately in manifestly grievous sin are not to be admitted to Holy Communion.[74]

The text appears unchanged, as can. 915, in the final text promulgated by Pope John Paul II.

The text of the canon is clear. Those under the imposed or declared ecclesiastical penalties of interdict and excommunication, and those who obstinately persist in manifest grave sin are not to be given Holy Communion. The text

---

[73] Pontificia Commisso Codici Iuris Canonici Recognoscendo, *Relatio complectens* (cf. nt. 71), 214

[74] Can. 913. *Codex Iuris Canonici: Schema Novissimum post consultationem S.R.E. Cardinalium, Episcoporum Conferentiarum, Dicasteriorum Curiae Romanae, Universitatum Facultatumque ecclesiasticarum necnon Superiorum Institutorum vitae consecratae recognitum, iuxta placita Patrum Commissionis deinde emendatum atque Summp Pontifici praesentatum,* E Civitate Vaticana 1982, 167

makes it clear that the Church has the responsibility to deny Holy Communion to those who are known to be under the imposed or declared penalties of excommunication and interdict, and to those who are known to persist obstinately in manifest grave sin. Although the text does not state so explicitly, it is clear that the Church's responsibility is carried out by the minister of Holy Communion.

Regarding those who obstinately persist in manifest grave sin, it is necessary to know that indeed the person does obstinately persist, that is, that his pastor has informed him about the grave and public sinfulness of what he is doing and has cautioned him about not approaching to receive Holy Communion. The commentary on the 1983 *Code of Canon Law*, prepared by the Canon Law Society of Great Britain and Ireland, summarizes the point:

> Likewise excluded are those "who obstinately persist in manifest grave sin." In this third case, unlike the first two, there has been no public imposition or declaration of the person's state and so, before a minister can lawfully refuse the Eucharist, he must be certain that the person obstinately persists in a sinful situation or in sinful behavior that is manifest (i.e. public) and objectively grave.[75]

Clearly, the burden is on the minister of Holy Communion who, by the nature of his responsibility, must prevent anything which profanes the Blessed Sacrament and endangers the salvation of the soul of the recipient and of those scandalized by his unworthy reception of Holy Communion.

---

[75] *The Canon Law Letter & Spirit: A Practical Guide to the Code of Canon Law*, Dublin, 1995, 503

What about the question of scandal? The safeguarding of the sacred necessarily means avoiding scandal. In its properly theological sense, scandal is an objective word, action, or omission which leads others into wrong thoughts, actions, or omissions.

John M. Huels, the commentator on can. 915 in the *New Commentary on the Code of Canon Law*, commissioned by the Canon Law Society of America, reduces scandal to a subjective reality, ignoring its essential connection to what is objective, what is right and wrong. He states:

> The fact of actual scandal is, moreover, culturally relative. What causes scandal in one part of the world may not cause scandal elsewhere. In North America the faithful often are more scandalized by the Church's denial of sacraments and sacramentals than by the sin that occasions it, because it seems to them contrary to the mercy and forgiveness commanded by Christ.[76]

If a word, an action, or an omission leads another into error or sin, there is scandal, whether the person who is led astray knows that he has been scandalized or not. If, as the commentator suggests, the faithful in North America believe that persons who publicly and grievously sin should be admitted to Holy Communion and that it would be wrong to deny to them the Sacrament, then effectively the faithful have been scandalized, that is, they have been led to forget or to disregard what the perennial discipline of the Church, beginning with Saint Paul's admonition to the Corinthians, has always remembered and safeguarded. This

[76] J.P. Beal., J.A. Coriden, and T.J. Green (eds.), *New Commentary on the Code of Canon Law*, New York, 2000, 1111

is not the scandal to which can. 855 §2, of the Pio-Benedictine *Code* refers.

Two kinds of error are involved. One has to do with the supreme holiness of the Eucharist, that is, the necessity to be well-disposed before approaching to receive the Sacrament. The other regards the objective moral evil of the acts which the person is known to have committed. Giving Holy Communion to one who is known to be a serious sinner leads people astray in two ways. Either they are led to think that it is not wrong for an unrepentant sinner to receive Holy Communion (and to be given the Holy Eucharist), or they are led to think that what the person is known to have done was not gravely sinful.

CHAPTER 10

Code of Canons
of the Eastern Churches

T he first draft of the canons regarding divine worship
and, above all, the Sacraments *(Schema Canonum de
Cultu Divino et Praesertim de Sacramentis)* of the *Code
of Canons of the Eastern Churches,* not surprisingly, contained
a discipline similar to the discipline of the Latin Church,
regarding the exclusion of public and grievous sinners from
reception of the Holy Eucharist. Can. 47 read:

> The publicly unworthy, unless their repentance
> and correction has been established, are to be kept
> from participation in the Divine Eucharist.[77]

The draft of the canons was sent to the organs of consultation, that is, the Patriarchates and other Eastern Churches, the

---

[77] Can. 47. *Nuntia* 11 (1980), 91

Dicasteries of the Roman Curia, the Conferences of Bishops which have oriental hierarchs as members, the ecclesiastical universities and faculties of Rome, and others.[78]

As a result of the consultation, the draft canon 47 underwent two revisions. First, the phrase, "unless their repentance and correction has been established," was omitted, because it was held to be unnecessary. Second, the phrase, "from participation in the Divine Eucharist," was changed to "from reception of the Divine Eucharist."[79] No official explanation of the second change is given. No doubt, the change reflects the greater precision which also marked the drafting of the Latin Code, taking care not to confuse participation in the Holy Eucharist with reception of the Holy Eucharist.

The draft of the *Code of Canons of the Eastern Churches (Schema Codicis Iuris Canonici Orientalis),* sent with the blessing of the Roman Pontiff, to the Members of the Pontifical Commission for the Revision of Oriental Canon Law, on October 17, 1986, contained the canon as revised. Can. 708 read:

> The publicly unworthy are to be kept from the reception of the Divine Eucharist.[80]

The text of the discipline remained unchanged as can. 712 in the *Code of Canons of the Eastern Churches* promulgated by Pope John Paul II on October 18, 1990.

Father Victor J. Pospishil, in his commentary on the *Code of Canons of the Eastern Churches,* gives only one example of those to be denied Holy Communion, namely, the member of the faithful who contracts marriage with an Eastern

---

[78] *Nuntia* 15 (1982), 3

[79] *Nuntia* 15 (1982), 32

[80] Can. 708. *Nuntia* 24-25 (1987), 131

non-Catholic without the permission of his or her Catholic Bishop.[81] For the rest, he comments negatively on the denial of Holy Communion to the divorced and remarried, advocating "some better future solution."[82] His commentary makes no reference to the lists of those to be prevented from reception of Holy Communion, which are found in the fonts of can. 712, for example, the legislation of the Synod of 1736 of the Maronite Church.

Father George Nedungatt notes the following in his commentary on the language of the *Code of the Canons of the Eastern Churches:*

> The Latin word "arcere" means "to prevent from approaching, keep away, repulse" (OLD, s. v. 2).
> It is more than "to forbid."[83]

Can. 712 of the *Code of Canons of the Eastern Churches* is more lapidary in its formulation, but it expresses one and the same discipline found in can. 915 of the *Code of Canon Law.*

[81] V.J. Pospishil, *Eastern Catholic Church Law,* 2nd ed., Staten Island (New York), 1996, 400

[82] V.J. Pospishil, *Eastern Catholic Church Law* (cf. nt. 81), 400-401

[83] G. Nedungatt, *A Companion to the Eastern Code,* Rome, 1994, 182

CHAPTER 11

Declaration of
the Pontifical Council
for Legislative Texts

On June 24, 2000, the Pontifical Council for Legislative Texts, "in agreement with the Congregation for the Doctrine of the Faith and with the Congregation for Divine Worship and the Discipline of the Sacraments," issued a declaration making it clear that can. 915 applies to the faithful who are divorced and remarried. Referring to the text of 1 Cor 11:27, 29, the Declaration expresses the theological and canonical reasons of can. 915:

> In effect, the reception of the Body of Christ when one is publicly unworthy constitutes an objective harm to the ecclesial communion: it is a behavior that affects the rights of the Church and of all the faithful to live in accord with the exigencies of that communion. In the concrete case of the admission

to Holy Communion of faithful who are divorced and remarried, the scandal, understood as an action that prompts others towards wrongdoing, affects at the same time both the sacrament of the Eucharist and the indissolubility of marriage. That scandal exists even if such behavior, unfortunately, no longer arouses surprise: in fact it is precisely with respect to the deformation of the conscience that it becomes more necessary for pastors to act, with as much patience as firmness, as a protection to the sanctity of the Sacraments and a defense of Christian morality, and for the correct formation of the faithful.[84]

The Declaration contains the basic reasons for the discipline of can. 915 and indicates the serious implications of the application of can. 915 for the communion of the Church, which Pope John Paul II presented in *Ecclesia de Eucharistia*. It also treats the serious element of scandal, noting that the error of so many of the faithful in the matter confirms, in fact, the scandal, and the need of a patient but firm action on the part of the Pastors of the Church.

The Statement refers clearly to an objective situation of sin, "a behavior," and the "objective harm" caused when a person who exhibits such behavior is given Holy Communion. The Declaration explicitly addresses those who would say that to deny Holy Communion, in accord with the norm of can. 915, "it would be necessary to establish the presence of all the conditions required for the existence of mortal sin, including those which are subjective, necessitating a

---

[84] Pontificium Consilium De Legum Textibus, "Acta Consilii: Dichiarazione," *Communicationes* 32 (2000), 160. English translation from *L'Osservatore Romano, Weekly Edition in English*, 12 July 2000, 3-4

judgment of a type that a minister of Communion could not make *ab externo*" and "to verify an attitude of defiance on the part of an individual who had received a legitimate warning from the Pastor."[85] Such requirements would "render the norm inapplicable."[86]

A similar argument has been used to deny the application of can. 915 in the case of a Catholic politician who votes for legislation that gravely violates the natural moral law. For example, during the discussion of the matter prior to the meeting of the United States Conference of Catholic Bishops in June of 2004, after citing the teaching of the *Catechism of the Catholic Church* on the conditions necessary for a sin to be mortal, one Bishop wrote:

> Given the long-standing practice of not making a public judgment about the state of the soul of those who present themselves for Holy Communion, it does not seem that it is sufficiently clear that in the matter of voting for legislation that supports abortion such a judgment necessarily follows. The pastoral tradition of the Church places the responsibility of such a judgment first on those presenting themselves for Holy Communion.[87]

The opinion expressed effectively, in the language of the Declaration, would make it impossible to apply can. 915. It confuses the norm of can. 916 with the norm of can. 915 in a way which makes can. 915 superfluous.

[85] Pontificium Consilium De Legum Textibus, "Acta Consilii: I, Dichiarazione" (cf. nt. 85), 159

[86] Ibid., 160

[87] Bishop D. Wuerl, "Faith, Personal Conviction and Political Life," *Origins* 34 (2004), 40

The long-standing discipline of the Church requires that the minister of Holy Communion exercise discretion regarding the distribution of Holy Communion to those who persist in manifest and grievous sin. The exercise of such discretion is not a judgment on the subjective state of the soul of the person approaching to receive Holy Communion but a judgment regarding the objective condition of serious sin in a person who, after due admonition from his pastor, persists in cooperating formally with intrinsically evil acts like procured abortion. In the Encyclical Letter *Evangelium vitae,* Pope John Paul II made clear the Church's teaching regarding the obligation of a Catholic legislator, when he declared:

> Abortion and euthanasia, therefore, are crimes which no human law can make ratified. Laws of this kind not only do not bind the conscience; truly they gravely and expressly compel that the same be opposed because of repugnance to conscience.[88]

The fifth principle of Cardinal Joseph Ratzinger's memorandum, "Worthiness to Receive Holy Communion," makes it clear that a Catholic politician's formal cooperation in abortion or euthanasia, that is, "his consistently campaigning and voting for permissive abortion and euthanasia laws," constitutes an "objective situation of sin," and that, therefore, "he is not to present himself for Holy Communion until he brings to an end the objective situation of sin."[89]

---

[88] Pope John Paul II, Encyclical Letter *Evangelium vitae,* "On the Inviolable Good of Human Life," 25 March 1995, AAS 87 (1995), 486, n. 73a

[89] United States Conference of Catholic Bishops, "On Catholics in Political Life," *Origins* 34 (2004), 134

Conclusions

What conclusions can be drawn from the study of the history of the canonical discipline of denying Holy Communion to those who obstinately persist in public grave sin?

First of all, the consistent canonical discipline permits the administering of the Sacrament of Holy Communion only to those who are properly disposed externally and forbids it to those who are not so disposed, prescinding from the question of their internal disposition, which cannot be known with certainty.

Secondly, the discipline is required by the invisible bond of communion which unites us to God and to one another. The person who obstinately remains in public and grievous sin is appropriately presumed by the Church to lack the interior bond of communion, the state of grace, required to approach worthily the reception of the Holy Eucharist.

Thirdly, the discipline is not penal but has to do with the safeguarding of the objective and supreme sanctity of the Holy Eucharist and with caring for the faithful who would sin gravely against the Body and Blood of Christ, and for the faithful who would be led into error by such sinful reception of Holy Communion.

Fourthly, the discipline applies to any public conduct which is gravely sinful, that is, which violates the law of God in a serious matter. Certainly, the public support of policies and laws which, in the teaching of the Magisterium, are in grave violation of the natural moral law falls under the discipline.

Fifthly, the discipline requires the minister of Holy Communion to forbid the Sacrament to those who are publicly unworthy. Such action must not be precipitous. The person who sins gravely and publicly must, first, be cautioned not to approach to receive Holy Communion. The memorandum, "Worthiness to Receive Holy Communion," of Cardinal Joseph Ratzinger, in its fifth principle, gives the perennial pastoral instruction in the matter. This, in fact, is done effectively in a pastoral conversation with the person, so that the person knows that he is not to approach to receive Holy Communion and that, therefore, the distribution of Holy Communion does not become an occasion of conflict. It must also be recalled that "no ecclesiastical authority may dispense the minister of Holy Communion from this obligation in any case, nor may he emanate directives that contradict it."[90]

---

[90] Pontificium Consilium De Legum Textibus, "Acta Consilii: I, Dichiarazione," *Communicationes* 32 (2000), 161; English translation from *L'Osservatore Romano, Weekly Edition in English,* 12 July 2000, 4.

Finally, the discipline must be applied in order to avoid serious scandal, for example, the erroneous acceptance of procured abortion against the constant teaching of the moral law. No matter how often a Bishop or priest repeats the teaching of the Church regarding procured abortion, if he stands by and does nothing to discipline a Catholic who publicly supports legislation permitting the gravest of injustices and, at the same time, presents himself to receive Holy Communion, then his teaching rings hollow. To remain silent is to permit serious confusion regarding a fundamental truth of the moral law. Confusion, of course, is one of the most insidious fruits of scandalous behavior.

I am deeply aware of the difficulty which is involved in applying the discipline of can. 915. I am not surprised by it and do not believe that anyone should be surprised. Surely, the discipline has never been easy to apply. But what is at stake for the Church demands the wisdom and courage of shepherds who will apply it.

The United States of America is a thoroughly secularized society which canonizes radical individualism and relativism, even before the natural moral law. The application, therefore, is more necessary than ever, lest the faithful, led astray by the strong cultural trends of relativism, be deceived concerning the supreme good of the Holy Eucharist and the gravity of supporting publicly the commission of intrinsically evil acts. Catholics in public office bear an especially heavy burden of responsibility to uphold the moral law in the exercise of their office which is exercised for the common good, especially the good of the innocent and defenseless. When they fail, they lead others—Catholics and non-Catholics alike—to be deceived regarding the evils of procured abortion and other attacks on innocent and defenseless human life, on the integrity of human procreation, and on the family.

As Pope John Paul II reminded us, referring to the teaching of the Second Vatican Ecumenical Council, the Holy Eucharist contains the entire good of our salvation.[91] There is no responsibility of the Church's shepherds which is greater than that of teaching the truth about the Holy Eucharist, celebrating worthily the Holy Eucharist, and directing the flock in the worship and care of the Most Blessed Sacrament. Can. 915 of the *Code of Canon Law* and can. 712 of the *Code of Canons of the Eastern Churches* articulate an essential element of the shepherds' responsibility, namely, the perennial discipline of the Church by which the minister of Holy Communion is to deny the Sacrament to those who obstinately persevere in manifest grave sin.

---

[91] EdeE, 1b

ABOUT
CATHOLIC ACTION
FOR FAITH AND FAMILY

Catholic Action for Faith and Family was founded in 2006 as a lay organization inspired by the teachings of the Roman Catholic Church and dedicated to upholding and promoting the ideals of Christian Civilization. Our mission centers on the Catholic Faith and the divine institution of the family as the primary instruments for the restoration of Christian order and virtuous living.

A FAITHFUL ECHO MOVEMENT was launched in the Fall of 2019 and is based on the belief that the Church must be a guide for society in order to deeply influence the course of history. For that reason, it is our conviction that now is the time for Clergy and Laity to collaborate more closely than ever to restore the sacred trust that Catholicism once held as the Church Christ founded.

We believe that the twin towers of Catholic witness – Clergy and Laity – must work together to reestablish Christendom's precious endowment of spiritual, cultural, moral, and social values.

A FAITHFUL ECHO OF THE EUCHARIST CAMPAIGN - The USCCB's multi-year Eucharistic Revival program seeks to address the triple challenges of declining Mass attendance, lack of understanding of the Real Presence of Christ in the Eucharist and increasing religious disaffiliation. Their strategic plan is designed to emphasize the importance of a strong return to the Eucharist as the "source and summit" of who we are and of what we do as Catholics.

At Catholic Action for Faith and Family, we strongly believe that as the Eucharistic Revival unfolds, our own Faithful Echo of the Eucharist activities will galvanize participation by Laity and Clergy, as well as strengthen commitments to Mass attendance and the worthy reception of Holy Communion. We believe these Campaigns, in conjunction with His Eminence's clear-sighted book, will help clergy and faithful understand better the confusion and scandal that afflicts the Church's most precious gift of the Body and Blood, Soul and Divinity of Jesus Christ.

PRESENTS

A FAITHFUL ECHO MOVEMENT

*Uniting Clergy and Laity to be a
Beacon of Light in the World*

CatholicAction.org

Learn more and get involved
with A Faithful Echo Movement.